LOVE BEYOND GOD

LOVE BEYOND GOD

Meditations

ADAM LAWRENCE DYER

SKINNER HOUSE BOOKS
BOSTON

Copyright © 2016 by Adam Lawrence Dyer. All rights reserved. Published by Skinner House Books, an imprint of the Unitarian Universalist Association, a liberal religious organization with more than 1,000 congregations in the U.S. and Canada, 24 Farnsworth St., Boston, MA 02210–1409.

www.skinnerhouse.org

Printed in the United States

Cover design by Kathryn Sky-Peck
Cover art: "Untitled (Protection Pyramid)" by Adee Roberson, copyright © 2012, acrylic on canvas
Author photo: Tara Layman
Text design by Suzanne Morgan

print ISBN: 978-1-55896-777-9
eBook ISBN: 978-1-55896-778-6

6 5 4 3 2 1
18 17 16

Library of Congress Cataloging-in-Publication Data

Names: Dyer, Adam Lawrence, author.
Title: Love beyond God : meditations / by Adam Dyer.
Description: Boston : Skinner House Books, 2016.
Identifiers: LCCN 2016003251 (print) | LCCN 2016004490 (ebook) | ISBN
  9781558967779 (pbk. : alk. paper) | ISBN 9781558967786 ()
Subjects: LCSH: Spirituality--Unitarian Universalist Association. |
  Meditations.
Classification: LCC BX9841.3 .D94 2016 (print) | LCC BX9841.3 (ebook) | DDC
  242—dc23
LC record available at http://lccn.loc.gov/2016003251

For Charles and Edwina

CONTENTS

Introduction	ix
Love Beyond God	1
American Villanelle	3
The Nod	4
All Color in the Spectrum	6
We Are Jazz	8
This Rose	11
Dashiki	12
Black Church	14
The Voice	15
Black Male Body	16
African Prince	18
Do #BlackLivesMatter?	20
Orphaned in History	22
For Rekia	24
Respectability Is Dead	25
What Do We Believe In?	26
Adrift in My Faith	28
End of the Franchise	31

white boy running	32
Gentle Man	34
Healing	36
Salvation (Fourth Principle)	38
Call to Worship	40
Without Grasping	42
Held in the Passion	43
Cue	44
First Breath	45
A Piece of Whiteness	46
Pray	48
The Dance Between the Two	50
La danza entre los dos	51
Ode for the Ally	52
A Song of Brown Bodies	54
The inSpirit Series	59

INTRODUCTION

What does it mean to speak of a "love beyond God?" As a black man in the United States in the era of Black Lives Matter, and as a Unitarian Universalist, I must answer this question every day. I am constantly confronted with an assault of images that show black people like me suffering extreme brutality. I am personally challenged by social assumptions about my intellect, my body, and my ability simply because of the color of my skin. I must reconcile my sense of self with a world that paints me as the perpetual outsider, no matter my achievements. At the same time, my chosen faith tradition of Unitarian Universalism lifts up a soaring rhetoric about the inherent worth and dignity of all, personal responsibility and individual agency. These noble aspirations keep me affiliated. Yet Unitarian Universalist churches remain dominated by white identity and privilege. This faith community struggles to invite and retain those who sit outside of white, hetero-normative, able, middle-class, English-speaking social locations. In the ongoing national dialogue on race in particular, Unitarian Universalism has been conflicted to the point of inertia so that we end up playing catch up or worse, sitting on the sidelines when we should be leading. In the end, balancing my blackness with my Unitarian Universalism requires that I dive deep into a reservoir of hope that is replenished and inspired by those who have trod this liminal space before me. It also requires a creative and unwavering spiritual grounding that cannot be limited by conventional expression. I must live immersed in the spirit of a love that frequently needs to go "beyond God" simply to survive.

The "love beyond God" concept may feel less accessible to some who do not share my social location or don't have a connection to spiritual matters. I point this out as an honest acknowledgement of different worldviews, not as a judgment. Therefore, consider this an invitation to dialogue. There can be no kind of community and no reconciliation between divided and separate ideologies—about race or religion—until we actually get to know one another. *Love Beyond God* offers observations from the life of a black man of faith in the predominantly white Unitarian Universalist denomination. Some of the pieces strongly echo the statement that "Black Lives Matter" and some ask questions about this stance. Some of the pieces paint pictures of lives lived in the context of whiteness, while others ruminate on the role of faith in responding to the idea that "all lives matter." I hope to offer a perspective that may be unfamiliar or even jarring to some while at the same time serve as a great comfort to others who have longed to see words like these in print. Overall, the goal is to keep us all in community and to foster deeper understanding all around.

All non-white people must know how to navigate whiteness in order to survive in our modern world. We regularly have to do so at the expense of our cultural and familial identities so that we can achieve in careers, live in certain neighborhoods, and even acquire certain types of education. Part of the invitation in these pages, therefore, is to ask white people to spiritually invest in learning how to navigate non-whiteness by actually getting to know our experiences. All people, regardless of faith or race, can grow in their understanding and compassion by becoming more intimate with uniquely identified experiences such as mine, presented here. We can love one another, but we must actually see each other in our completeness first.

LOVE BEYOND GOD

What if every time you woke
Your sigh was felt
By every being on Earth?

What if every time you spoke
Your words were heard
By every ear on Earth?

What if when you told a joke
You tickled the senses
Of every smile on Earth?

What if with each tender stroke
You shared your touch
With every hand on Earth?

What if when your heart broke
You tasted the tears
Running down every cheek on Earth?

No bond or brand or "guilted" yoke,
Surely this is love that reaches beyond,
That holds one to another
And every other to one.
No matter the color
Or where we're from.

This is now.
This is we.
This is Love.
This is God.

And this is love beyond God.

AMERICAN VILLANELLE

Who are you to name my race?
Your words are only pale reflections
Of pride you wear about your face.

I danced with nature, found its grace.
You called it savage . . . not your predilection.
Who were you to name my race?

My body thrived throughout this place
But meeting you it learned infections,
Lesions that enflamed my face.

You killed my land and wasted space
And tried to give the earth directions.
Who were you to name my race?

Once, I nearly vanished . . . not a trace,
Invisible to all inspection;
Erased from all the planet face.

But lust propelled your forbears' chase
No contract bound their brute selection.
Yes, who are you to name my race,
When truth be told, you wear *my* face.

THE NOD

You've seen it. Two black men pass each other on the street. They nod. Subtle, sometimes imperceptible, but there *is* acknowledgement.

"Do you know him?"
"No . . . (yes)
. . . no."

I learned this from my father and my grandfather and my other grandfather and my uncles and my great uncle and from every other black man in my early life. Once, as a teenager, I didn't do it. I was verbally accosted from behind, "Don't you ever forget . . . *I'm all you've got!*" I've never forgotten since.

These days it gets harder. I walk through places where armies of broken black men inhabit the corners and wander aimless and beaten. When I cross their paths, I look for that acknowledgement, the one that says, "We are valid. We are real, we have a place, we have a family . . . *you are all I've got.*" When it doesn't come—obscured by drugs and desperation, or more often from just trying to live as part of this grand experiment called *America*, pressed down, shot at, torn apart, stolen from, talked about and not to, criminalized and caricatured—part of me dies inside.

The young brother passes without it. It is generational too. Fewer and fewer young people making this contact. I wonder if they really feel safe? So safe that they don't need this kind of community. Not just with skin color, but feeling no need to recognize each other for *any* reason. Maybe they are afraid because they see me as the unknown. *My God, we don't recognize each other!* Maybe we aren't teaching them that the struggle isn't over, that time hasn't healed a wound that opens, over and over again. That this simple acknowledgement . . . nod . . . was once all we had, and still, like it or not, *may be all we've got.*

ALL COLOR IN THE SPECTRUM

Chocolate,
Cocoa,
Caramel,
Sugar . . .
I am always described as food,
As if my skin is something that needs a filter
To make me even more delicious.
It was not the white man that named me this way . . .
I named myself as "dinner"
Like so many efforts to reclaim my body
That has been
Raped,
Castrated,
Flogged,
Objectified,
Used,
  . . . used up.

But in making myself tasty,
Have I diminished myself
To a fantasy for little minds
That can't cope with the fact that
Black is the presence of all color in the spectrum,
Or deal with the fact that I am, in one breath,
Enormous,
Vast as the whole of the African continent
Where my hues range from

Pale golden-eyed Arab
To ink-black Nigerian.
This must be the jealous racism
That cannot point to his skin and say,
"My ancestors *invented* civilization."

No, I should not compete with myself.
I know better.
It is all there in the ages of time that my skin portrays.
I am content to see my own
Dark, ruddy, burnished satin,
With no more beauty than your
Cinnamon-spattered eggshell.
Really, there is no real nourishment in skin color,
These are empty calories.
But there are stories and histories
And they have a beauty all their own.

WE ARE JAZZ

(1,2,3 . . .)

Just as soon as it began
We forgot how it started.
Like a Coltrane tune
We are so absorbed in trying to follow
To figure out
We forget that we are part of it.
Every tune needs ears
And every ear needs a tune.
Some let the sounds wash past them
And others are
Tapping
     Clapping
          Snapping
A slap happy chorus
Embodied instruments
Becoming part of the beat.

"Jazz is a heartbeat . . . its heartbeat is yours"
Said Langston,
Played Mingus,
Sang Ella.
The sound that swings, blues and rocks,
Is us,
Is U-S.
Its dissonance is our politics

Its harmony, our dream.
The drum thumps brutal as the master's whip
The cymbals sizzle like Native bodies ablaze
The saxophones wail and climax like rape
The horns push their Musical Destiny
While the bass bubbles underneath like God,

Underscoring the only true sounds,

Nature and time.

Improbable
Unfathomable
Unconscionable
Unconscious

The United States of Otherness
We are jazz.
African rhythm
Played on European instruments
Toying with Asian harmonies
In a language made of Middle Eastern letters
While standing on the First People's land
Where none of us belongs.
Yet that is the brutal beauty of any combo
Because the instruments are not alike,
The players are individuals,
None of them belong where they are
And none of them belong together.
A Dixieland chorus of separate lines
Just lucky to be in the same key, in the same room.

Yet they make the most beautiful music
With depth, range, beauty, heart.

Hearty . . . "Chop Suey."

Jazz is a heartbeat,
Our heartbeat is jazz.

THIS ROSE

The purpose of the open flower
is not about the present hour,
instead it hints at legacies
and beauty's hope for what can be.

We too are called to be the flower
that buds along the fragile bower,
where beauty, hope, and what can be,
for now, may be but filigree.

So where the rose in spring may flower,
bathed in sun and quenched by shower,
we grow to show posterity
bright blooming through adversity.

DASHIKI

The colors are so vivid.
Yellow, blue, green, gold, white . . .
And red.
Red background,
Red sleeves,
Red body,
Behind the etch-a-sketch design
Around the neck,
And at the cuffs.
Bright colors
Outlined in black.
A million-legged creature
Swimming from Ghana
Up my chest,
Down my back,
Around the collar
In perfect, tidy, delicate rows.
This was all mine.

It is imprinted in my memory
Along with the rest of 1971,
When black still had power
And an afro was a statement
And "gimme five" was only a black thing.
The smell of mom's hot comb
Was already a fading memory,
Traded for a pick and AfroSheen.

While Dad swapped "high and tight"
For sideburns, a turtleneck, and beaded chains.
Aretha, Stevie, Sly, Marvin, Roberta Flack
Gave my world its soundtrack,
And even if we didn't know exactly what it was,
Or actually believe it could be true,
We kids *looked* like we had black power.

I miss my six-year-old self.
I had black power.
I didn't question my 'fro,
I didn't doubt my beauty or my brain,
I didn't have to ponder my skin.

I was proud of my dashiki.

BLACK CHURCH

Whether large and formal
or shabby and small,
there is pride here that is palpable
and voices that call.

Yes, you belong. Step inside.

You have been burdened . . . rest.
You have been tried . . . breathe.
You have cried . . . laugh.
You have been silenced . . . sing.

Sing . . .

And that song is what you remember,
the one that some adopt,
and others co-opt.
It is the voice of community,
it is the sound of an embrace,
it is the music of unconditional,
unfiltered,
unframed,
and unparalleled love
born of struggle and nurtured on hope.

Sing . . .
and bring your whole self,
large and formal or shabby and small.
Your voice is always welcome in this song.

THE VOICE
(for Ta-Nehisi Coates)

I think you know me.
No, I think you really,
    really,
        know me.

Each word you write
is like water on a rag in the sun.
I soak them up
and thirst for more.

I am so terribly dry,
parched,
from the blazing scrutiny
from being wrung
by the every day twisting inquiry
from bleached blind eyes,
always asking "Who am I?"

 . . . so tired of answering.
I want someone to just "know"
    You know?
        Like you know me.

BLACK MALE BODY

Potent.
You cannot understand my potency
If you only see my body.
Yes, I know . . . I am beautiful.
You long to touch, taste, smell, succumb
To what you see as brutal and raw.
I am the black male body.

Primitive.
Ha . . . but my "primitive" is
Too sophisticated for your palette
Too rich for your belly
Too delicate for your nose.
I am the black male body.

I have been both prison and palace,
Prisoner and prince,
King and conquered,
Kin and concubine,
And surely my history predates you
For where would "Eve" be without "Adam"?
Yes, she birthed the world
But I set her on fire.
We devoured each other in our own big bang
 . . . together we made humanity.

I am the black male body.
But I am not just sex.

I am not just your perversion of pieces.
I am not a tool poised to penetrate at will.
I am my own pain and joy,
Dreams and anguish.
I am love and war,

And I am not you.

I speak in languages you can't imagine,
Dance to rhythms you'll never hear,
Sing songs in harmony
That you can only try to get near.
My magic so slick
You don't even know it's a trick.
Yes, I am all that *and* a lover.
I am the black male body.

AFRICAN PRINCE

Do NOT touch my hair.

I am not your "African Prince."
I could not be your African Prince,
Because you have no idea what Africa
Or princes
Actually look like.

As you grab for my hair,
MY hair
Atop MY head,
My "crown"
That holds my history . . .
Lost friends,
Lived places,
Loved bodies . . .
As you reach out to touch
My hair . . . my story
You only want to connect
To your myth of me
And continue the age-old assault.

In that one childlike gesture,
You become a dangerous shadow to me,
A fading picture of what once was.
The slug of your own life's moisture
Sapped by the salt world of men.
A faded list of entitlements and rights

That silently laid claim to everything around you,
Clutching at what it could find,
Among them . . . my very being.

Did you miss it?
I crossed myself off that list.
I broke those chains,
I learned to speak your language
And remembered my own.
Pointed your direction and said
In the universal tongue,

"NO!"

Do NOT touch my hair.
I am not your African Prince
Nor your Nubian Maiden
Or exotic Indian brave
Hot blooded Latin spice
Or condiment of any kind
To be sprinkled on the main course of your life.

I am a vital human man
Of blood and breath,
Sinew and semen,
Art, hope, passion,

And quickly fading patience.

DO #BLACKLIVESMATTER?

On voting day,
Thanks to the casual Supreme Court erasure
Of one hundred years of struggle for suffrage,
Tangled restrictions and loopholes
Will block the opportunity
For large pockets of American black people
To make their voices heard in a government
That only really wanted three-fifths of them anyhow
 . . . do #blacklivesmatter?

On protest day,
When a white police officer
Shot and killed a black teenager;
And the officer walked free,
Tension builds just below the boiling point.
And nothing will be done.
It will not spill over, or truly ignite,
Once again, the intense heat will just burn itself out
From four hundred years of battle fatigue
 . . . do #blacklivesmatter?

On sentencing day,
A million black men will look across at faces
In "cells" and "pens,"
Hating each other, hating themselves
For being made into animals by forced desperation.
An entire generation screaming for validation and truth.

But they are left mute . . . their vocal cords cut
By a white washed system of "justice."
 . . . do #blacklivesmatter?

On Thanksgiving Day,
Black people will swarm the commercial circus.
Target, Walmart, Nordstrom . . .
Searching for some way to reflect a sense of self.
Forced in the end to buy warped images
From the fun-house mirrors
Put in place by the capitalist ring master
Who still only sees a price tag when he sees their bodies.
 . . . do #blacklivesmatter?

White people . . . Do black lives matter?
Black people . . . Do black lives matter?
America . . . Do black lives matter?
World . . . Do black lives matter?
It is voting day, and it is judgment day.

#blacklivesmatter.

ORPHANED IN HISTORY

I struggle with history,
The flickering yellowed images,
The faded pages,
The fond memories,
Nostalgia.
The Ken Burns pan-and-scan of faces,
Documentary
After documentary,
Are not what I am looking for.
These images are more distant,
More removed,
Disconnected from me
By handlebar mustaches,
And porcelain skin.
These recollections,
This fondness for painting the past,
Does not even know I existed,
. . . except for slavery
And the Reverend Dr. King.
And so, this "history"
Is "their"-story.
It does not belong to me,
I did not tell it,
I did not write it,
I do not own it,
I do not want it.

Who *will* tell my story
Beyond the color lines,
Beyond the lunch counters,
Beyond the chains
Of slavery and jails?
Who will tell stories
Older than two millennia,
Of kings and goddesses,
Legends and legacies,
That blend and bend
In a portrait that traces my profile
And tinges my brow?
Who will tell *my* history,
When and how?

FOR REKIA

We see you.
We see you, Rekia Boyd.
That night, thinking, "I'm alright."
That day, feeling, "I am loved."

We see you . . .

We do not need to know you to see you,
Because we too were once twenty-two.
And just like you, we knew we were invincible.
Funny wasn't just funny . . . it was a riot.
Nights didn't end, they turned into dawn.
And friends were forever,
And love was a weekend or two.

At least we hope that's how it was for you . . .

Yes, we see you, Rekia Boyd.
We see you, good choices and bad.
We see you, in a crowd.
We see you, alone.
You are alright.
You are loved,
And we pray that the world can see and love you too.

RESPECTABILITY IS DEAD

A strident voice rises during the speech, making for an awkward pause, nervous glances, a rustle in the crowd. . . . The words of protest begin in earnest, ringing out as a last pleading gasp of someone's unending oppression and pain. The voice is charged, electrified, fully exposed, ready to shock, yet naked and vulnerable to being defused by bullies and boos. These are the words that must be said from the voices that are either silent or silenced. Here, unanticipated, unwanted, they rise, hijacking attention, saying, "I will not be un-heard." And the words come alive. They are unavoidably present, announcing that the movement and the moment are unquestionably now.

WHAT DO WE BELIEVE IN?

Do not struggle with what you have,
Fighting for a word called "prosperity,"
Dancing with a concept called "mobility,"
Searching for a place called "security."

Believe that you have enough.

easy to say when your belly is full,
when you are warm and dry,
and when smiles are affirmation . . .

> *less when pockets are empty*
> *and you fear failure every day*
> *in a place where every face is another debt to pay*

Do not struggle with how you are,
Fighting for the perfect body,
Dancing with identity,
Searching for peaceful physicality,

Believe that you are enough.

easy to say when your body behaves,
when the mirror reflects desire
and you are the light of beauty and youth . . .

> *less when each breath brings agony*
> *and your body is a ship,*
> *navigating between pain and limitation*

Do not struggle with how you feel,
Fighting for laughter,
Dancing with humor,
Searching for joy,

Believe that you feel enough.

easy to say when you are connected
and there are shoulders to cry on
and hands to hold . . .

> *less when bleakness surrounds you*
> *when your only "friend" is sleep*
> *and sleep is as elusive as a lover*

But you must believe

You have enough.
You are enough.
You feel enough.

If *you* don't believe . . . no one else will.
The first step to being loved

Is believing you can love yourself.

ADRIFT IN MY FAITH

Sometimes I am adrift in my faith,
All at sea.
I must remind myself that not only can I swim,
But I can read the sun and the moon.
I know the smell of the storm on the horizon,
And the buzz of the fly that says, "land ho!"

I am adrift, and I am nearer the shore than my parents
Or my ancestors,
Shadowy figures from books
Whose battered and used-up bodies
Manage to lift me above the waves
To breathe the sweet sea air.
Though waves will rise as high as my brow,
I am able to hold my breath until they ebb
And I can breathe in the sun again.

I am adrift,
All around me an ocean.
I am a land creature by nature
I have no gills or fins or scales
And my blood is warm.
This ocean could consume me
With its temperature,
Its toxicity;
Asphyxiating,
Dehydrating.

It is not my natural element
But it is beautiful and enticing;
An endless plane of silken ultramarine
Piqued in white lace.
It enfolds me every so often
In an embrace.
And I rest, but briefly.

I am adrift.
And the silken sea water glance across my skin
Can send a chill
Or lap at my neck.
Much too close, despite its vast expanse.
Oh, how I long for dry land,
dry . . . safe . . . land,
Placing my feet on terra firma,
Terra familiar, where I know I can stand
And be seen with my face turned up to the sun, saying,
"Yes! I know I am not a fish!"
I am not the "other,"
I am human and I can swim.

So, I am adrift.
Held aloft by my forebears
Standing above the waves
Walking on water.
I read the sun and the moon
And brace for the storm on the horizon
And lead the way home.

For I have heard the fly buzz,
It is the sound that excites my ear.
I can hear
Ever so tiny and clear,

>(. . . listen)

>> . . . *land ho!*

END OF THE FRANCHISE

You have to make your peace with the chaos, but you cannot lie. You cannot forget how much they took from us and how they transfigured our very bodies into sugar, tobacco, cotton, and gold.
—*Ta-Nehisi Coates*

Is this what the end of the old "white man franchise" looks like? The stores all seem to be empty now and the shelves are bare. There is still a lot to do before the crew clears the site for a school or a house of worship or a farm: *A place where things will grow.* The building must be razed, foundation broken up, plumbing dismantled, and the toxic land replaced with fertile soil.

For now, though, a few last customers still come, desperate for one more deal. They hang on to the hope that just around the corner, in the next aisle, they will see the last Christmas ornaments . . . the one remaining Barbie doll . . . the final flag . . . the leftover pistol . . . that everyone else missed. Something to make the trip worth the trouble. They came so far to this place they were told would always be here, and suddenly, it is no more. It is raining outside too and the roads have become dark and slick. There are no lights, and all the cops they could trust are gone. Getting home will be even more treacherous, depending on how fast they choose to drive. I pray they get home safely.

But tomorrow the demo begins. The vision comes anew. The plans have been laid. Let the wrecking ball swing.

WHITE BOY RUNNING

The phenomenon of Berkeley springtime:
College-age white boys running . . . everywhere.

beautiful
you are called beautiful
you are the embodiment of every freedom in america
your body drips with the world's envy
glinting young elastic muscles
rebounding every stride
golden boldness
shock in the sun
all american dream
wrapped in you
rapt by you
hypnotic
as you run down streets
run around cars
run past signs
never looking
never care
beautiful american
beautiful freedom
beautiful white male youth

traffic crowds reason
the world parts for you like moses
stops for you like time
waits for you like the messiah

danger fear doubt
do not count
no need for obama,
you are the definition of hope
and you are beautiful

but where are you going
what are you running from
is that careless pride
    or panic in your gait
is that unbridled joy
    or jealousy in your face
do your arms swing for balance
    or strike at a world as yet to be defined
if you truly believed your beauty
    would you work so hard to leave others behind
and you stumble now along the trail
of red white and blue
trying to fill the enormous strides
of an impossible outdated dream
still drunk on the pheromones of pride

what if you just stopped
would you die
would you be caught
would you see that this race
is only you
beautiful white boy

running against yourself and against time

GENTLE MAN

Gentle man, shower me
Be the rain
Not raging storms
Or thundering skies
But gentle man, feeding rivers
When gently you flow.

Gentle man, sway with me
Be the wind
Not raging gale
Or roaring twister
But gentle man, leaning forests
When gently you blow.

Gentle man, hold me
Be the ocean
Not under current
Or ripped tide
But gentle man, molding shores
When gently you undertow.

Gentle man, shine on me
Be the sun
Not blinding rays
Or searing heat
But gentle man, warming golden harvests
When gently you glow.

So, gentle man, love me
Be elemental
Not brutal hand
Or selfish heart
But gentle man, planting seeds of truth
That gently, gently grow.

HEALING

Don't speak to me of "healing" racism,
or "wounded souls" or the "painful hurt"
until you are willing to feel the scars
on my great-great-grandmother Laury's back.

Don't speak to me of "values"
or "justice" or "righting wrongs"
until you are able to feel the heartache
of my great-grandfather Graham
whose father may have been his master.

Don't speak to me of "equity"
or "opportunity" or the "common good"
until you are able to hear the fear
from my grandmother Mae
as the only black woman in her college.

Don't speak to me of "passion"
or "longing" or "standing on the side of love"
until you know the shame
felt by my mother Edwina
mocked by teachers for the curve of her back.

Don't speak to me of "together"
or "understanding" or "empathy"
until you know my rage
as a young actor hearing the direction
to "be more *black* . . . more *male*."

The pain you are trying to heal has no real name.
This "pain" you speak of has no story;
it is anonymous, vague, and empty.

Don't speak to me of "healing"
for I heal the second I am ripped apart.
My wounds self-suture,
and like the clever creature I am,
I just grow new legs to outrun the pain ever faster.
It is something I have had to practice for generations,
that feel like an eternity.

So, please don't speak to me of "healing"
because you cannot know what healing means
until you know the hurt.

SALVATION (FOURTH PRINCIPLE)

Bring your cross to this chalice,
weighty symbol of faith
heavy with meaning,
love and hate.
Sign of hope and instrument of death.
The cross comes with you and all you bring to this chalice.

Bring your burden to this chalice,
all the dark and tragic past,
genocide and death,
justified by government.
Both horror and herald all in the name of God.
The burden comes with you and all you bring to this chalice.

Bring your "sin" to this chalice,
bring the worst that you can do.
All the guilt and doubt and fear
where the price for eternal life in death,
feels like a living hell.
Your "sin" comes with you and all you bring to this chalice.

Bring your shame to this chalice,
secret passions, misplaced desires,
oppression in the worst degree,
children, women, men in pain,
at the hands of those who should bring ease.
Your shame comes with you and all you bring to this chalice.

But also bring your love to this chalice.
Bring your joy and bring your adulation.
Stand for the "least of these."
Feed the multitudes with seven loaves,
demand truth at the altar of peace,
let no one go hungry.
Your love comes with you and all you bring to this chalice.

So, bring your cross to this chalice.
For the flame that burns in the bowl,
is not the flame to set your past alight
or to immolate what was not right.
But the flame that makes your hopes ignite,
and feeds the flame in which we all delight.

CALL TO WORSHIP

"Praise Jesus!"
The shouts are sometimes loud
Sometimes subtle
Personal
Reassuring
Proclaiming
Public
Private . . .
Intoned with voices that have richness and timbre,
Full with history and deeply lived life.

He sits in the pew feeling outside of himself,
Knowing everyone can see
That he doesn't belong here.
"The Spirit" is not in him.
Even though he tries to find *It* every single time,
It does not come.

And the church ladies
Who regard him
From beneath their brims
And over their collars,
Walking profusions of fuchsia and lilac, canary and rose,
And white . . .
Looking through him, he knows *they know* . . .

>   *"Sinner!"*

They had a dream.

They only want to see him as they dreamed he would be.
They only feel for what they hoped he would become:
The tall, black savior affirming their blood and sweat.

"But he was such a nice boy . . ."

So he sits in the pew, disembodied from his skin
Heart aching from the disappointment
That they all project on him
Damning everything he really is
Missing every blessing he'll become.

WITHOUT GRASPING

I adore you
you are my bird.
But as with any winged creature
I must hold you with open fingers
knowing that you are meant to fly.
I live for your warmth in my palm
but I am breathless at your beauty in the sky.
Fly, my bird, fly.
I adore you
in my hand
or on high.

HELD IN THE PASSION

Awaken now
Cradled in God's love.
Here, there is total ecstasy.
Arm draped about waist
Head in the crook of shoulder
Feet and legs entwined
Warmth igniting skin
In and around
With a yearning beyond bodies.
Hair entangled turning,
Breath pungent with the odor of time
The smell of holiness, wholeness,
Safety and sacredness.
Drawing closer,
Aroused and drowsy,
Enflamed heart pounding with anticipation,
Pulsing flushed neck burning for this perfect kiss.
Aching to yield.
Never forsaken.

CUE

She leaps out into the intersection, more concerned with her ballet arms than with staying alive. Her parents look the other way, with a laugh at some private joke that speaks to their solid intimacy. The little girl skips and dances across the street, wearing shorts that are fine now, on an eight-year-old body. But the same shorts and manner may send a different message when she is twenty. She's already learning to be unfettered, independent, and free, and so she always will be.

You might look at this and say, "Of course, all children should be this way!" But what is the pattern? She's already been told that she's pretty. She's already been instructed to look for a "prince," because she is Daddy's princess (whatever that is) and her "strong, independent" mother still prioritizes "him and his" over her own needs. The little girl sees, and learns.

When they walk, as they pass the Black Man, Daddy places his hand on the little girl in an unconscious gesture, but one that is real just the same. He's unaware, still laughing with his wife, but the little girl gets the cue and looks sheepishly at the Black Man. She stops skipping. The Black Man doesn't see the family. He is headed to perform surgery, or lead litigation, or maybe to save the world. No matter. In that moment, he has become "Black Man," permanently connected to the protective hand of Daddy, and the target of a weary stare from underneath the suspicious brow of an eight-year-old who just learned her first racial cue.

FIRST BREATH

That first breath must be delicious.

It must be more tantalizing,
more intoxicating than any drug,
fragrant like no flower will ever be
enticing like no body scent.
It must be all of this, and more
yet without words or memories, how do we know?

That first glorious rush of air
wants us to keep breathing
wants our hearts to keep beating
wants our eyes to open and see
wants our souls to open and say "yes."

The first breath wants us to live all our life saying,
please God,
let me live
let me breathe
for just one day more
until we breathe our very last.

A PIECE OF WHITENESS

She thought by holding you,
She could have a piece of whiteness,
A piece of the dream.
By seeing her reflection in your eyes
Hers would somehow turn blue,
Or by caressing your skin
Hers would turn pink.
That somehow
You would rub off on her.

She thought being in your life
Her life would turn to whiteness as well,
And that she would magically take on
The cloak of security
The walk of serenity
The chin of arrogance.
By mere association,
She would be safe.
She thought she could have a piece of whiteness.

But you only hold her as a dare.
You see her as foreign.
She is all thrill and danger and "other"
And although there is love
She is not *the* love.
For you, she is mostly
"Not whiteness."

It slips from her fingers,
And fades from her view,
When suddenly you see yourself
And find a thrill in your mirror image
When you walk with yourself
And know community.
Whiteness escapes her
When it joins you.
All she holds is loss
All she feels is pain
All that's left is empty
And that becomes her whiteness.

PRAY

How will *you* pray for *me*?
Will you summon *your* God
Will you call on *your* symbols
Will you tell me *your* ritual
Is that all you can say?
How will you pray?

How will you pray for me?
When you see me in chains,
Will you judge
Will you jury
Will you sentence my stay?
How will you pray?

How will you pray for me?
When my head is covered and yours is bare,
If my language is ancient
And yours barely there.
If my best day of rest
Is your longest day of play,
How will you pray?

How will you pray for me?
Will you see my skin,
Will you feel my body,
Will you know my mind?
Will you understand my words,
Or will you try to always place them

In *your* particular order and way?
How will you pray?

How will you pray for me?
If I don't pray at all,
If I am not called or calling
Deemed or damaged,
If I see myself not broken
But beautiful every day,
How will you pray?

And if you've never prayed,
And if you don't have the time,
And if you see faith as sanctified crime,
And too high a price for your sense of self to pay,
Can you still look into my eyes
Hold my joy or hear my cries?
Can you love me,
Love me,
Love me,
Love me just enough
In your own way
And pray?

THE DANCE BETWEEN THE TWO
(on Día de muertos)

From the darkness there is light,
After day there is night,
So the sun chases the moon
And so we live and so we die.
But if we carry heavy hearts,
Let the spirits of our departed
Lift us up and help us fly.
Mix our tears with their laughter
Blend our joy with their memory.
Let the living dance with the dead
So that we all may rest in peace
With the beauty and wholeness of our lives.
For just as the sun chases the moon,
It is the dance between the two
That brings the golden break of dawn
And exquisite purple twilight.

LA DANZA ENTRE LOS DOS
(en Día de muertos)

De la oscuridad surge la luz,
después del día viene la noche,
así el sol persigue a la luna
y así vivimos y morimos.
Pero si nos pesa el corazón,
dejemos que los espíritus de quienes se han ido
nos levanten, nos ayuden a volar.
Mezclemos nuestras lágrimas con sus risas
nuestra alegría con su memoria.
Dejemos que los vivos dancen con los muertos
Para que todos podamos descansar en paz
con la belleza y la plenitud de nuestras vidas.
Porque así como el sol persigue a la luna
Es la danza entre los dos lo que
trae el dorado despuntar del alba
y un exquisito crepúsculo púrpura.

traducción de Tania Marquez

ODE FOR THE ALLY

Must each interaction be drenched in guilt?
Must every question be met with a stopping hand?
Must every statement be met with suspicion?

Where is my peace?

Must every tear be questioned in its heart?
Must every action be challenged as true?
Must every joy be met with a new sorrow?

Where is my peace?

My piece understands the pain
    but cannot feel it.
My piece hears the cry
    but cannot translate it.
My piece knows the sorrow
    but cannot relieve it.

Because, I must also own my piece
As the boot
As the barrier
And the barrel
None of which I wield
Yet all of which I hold in the history of my face.

So, I seek to make my peace
With my boots in the streets
Where I pull down barriers

And stand before barrels 'til they fire or fall
Trumpeting the call of witness
Declaring "Enough!"
Especially when I am in the shadow of privilege
Or tucked away in those secret safe inside places
Where I am right up against the ear
Of those who have *all* the pieces.

This is my piece.
This is my peace.

A SONG OF BROWN BODIES

Each morning I wake
And see "me" as one of many

> *Brown bodies*
> *Brown bodies*

And my own skin and hair
Has the same shadows and light
As what I see online . . .

> *Brown bodies*
> *Brown bodies*

Lifeless and limp
Or trying but failing to flee
Battered and broken . . . never free

Could be me . . .

> *Brown bodies*
> *Brown bodies*

Scattered in streets
Grotesque golliwogs
Raggedy animated
By "white" imagination
Like puppets . . . playthings
For the progeny of hate

> *Brown bodies*
> *Brown bodies*

Used for a target, tune, or fuck
Diversions of passion
Co-opted visions
The promise of "change"

> *Brown bodies*
> *Brown bodies*

Living on the wrong side of "gentrified"
A fetish for the hipster "dark side"
Always "columbused" then ghettoized

> *Brown bodies*
> *Brown bodies*

Sacrificed to places
Where water poisons
And viruses thrive . . .

Where language fails
And walls rise . . .

Where war rages
And rape cries . . .

Where profit outpaces peace
And hope dies

> *Brown bodies*
> *Brown bodies*

Yet, the blessed curse
Of genetic fecundity

Means no onslaught of nature
Or man-made conflict
Or in-bred hatred
Can delete the DNA
That comes back for more,
Millennium and again.
It is the human penchant
For pandemic procreativity
That means there will always be

> *Brown bodies*
> *Brown bodies*

Do not believe what we are taught to be.
Each morning we all must arise
To see ourselves among the many

> *Brown bodies*
> *Brown bodies*

Embracing these colors of earth
Breathing the sigh of the sky
Quaking with the power of mountains alive
And feeling the spray of oceans
As we rise to celebrate

> *Brown bodies*
> *Brown bodies*

Where dance is blood
Where song is vision
Where touch is art

Where rhythm of heart
Pulses through words
And tumbles in rhyme,
Lovingly schooling the wicked
And scorning the vainly wise.

These are the real

> *Brown bodies*
> *Brown bodies*

Each one is precious
And holds the legacy
Of what it means to be wholly alive in

> *Brown Bodies*
> *Brown Bodies*

THE INSPIRIT SERIES

Unitarians and Universalists have been publishing collections of prayers and meditations for more than 175 years. In 1841 the Unitarians broke with their tradition of publishing only formal theology and released *Short Prayers for the Morning and Evening of Every Day in the Week, with Occasional Prayers and Thanksgivings*. Over the ensuing years, the Unitarians published many more volumes of prayers, including Theodore Parker's selections. In 1938, *Gaining a Radiant Faith* by Henry H. Saunderson launched the tradition of an annual Lenten manual.

Several Universalist collections appeared in the early nineteenth century as well. A comprehensive *Book of Prayers* was published in 1839, featuring both public and private devotions. Like the Unitarians, the Universalists published Lenten manuals, and in the 1950s they complemented this series with Advent manuals.

In 1961, the year the Unitarians and Universalists consolidated, the Lenten manual evolved into a meditation manual. And in 2015, reflecting a renewed vision for a wider audience, the name evolved once again into the inSpirit series.

> For a complete list of titles in the inSpirit series,
> please visit **uua.org/inspirit**